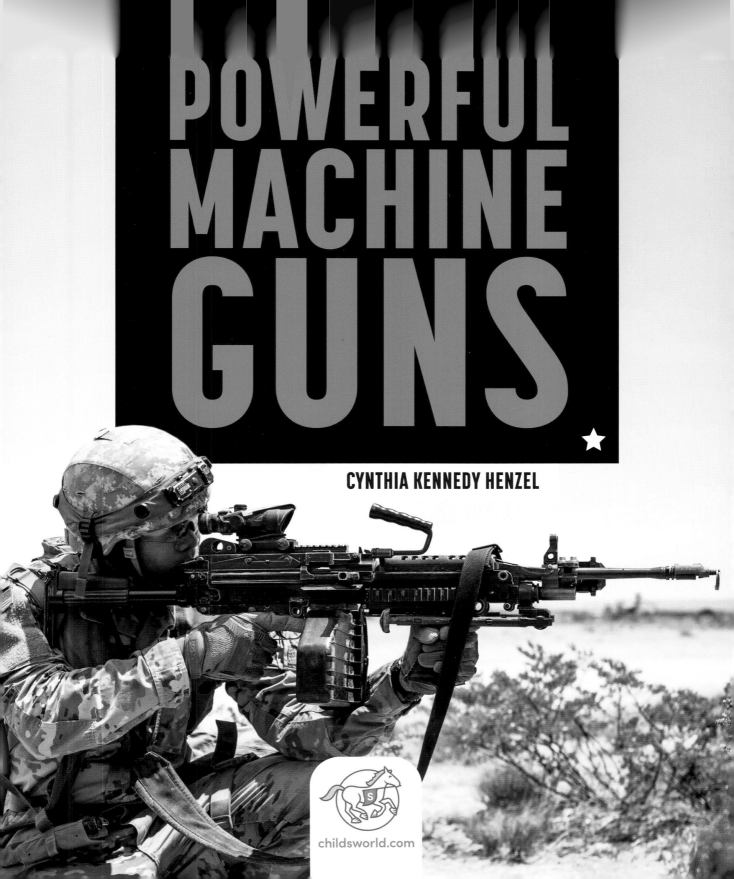

POWERFUL MACHINE GUNS

CYNTHIA KENNEDY HENZEL

childsworld.com

The Child's World®
childsworld.com

Published by The Child's World®
800-599-READ • www.childsworld.com

Photography Credits
Photographs ©: Spc. Tin P. Vuong/1st Armored Division
Combat Aviation Brigade/DVIDS, cover, 1; Lance Cpl. Scott
Aubuchon/US Marine Corps/US Navy, 3; Maj. Thomas
Piernicky/4th Sustainment Command (Expeditionary)/
DVIDS, 5; Thomas Alvarez/Idaho Army National Guard/
DVIDS, 7, 21 (middle); Pfc. Cameron Boyd/US Army/
Department of Defense, 9; Justin Connaher/Joint Base
Elmendorf-Richardson Public Affairs/DVIDS, 10; Lance
Cpl. Brienna Tuck/31st Marine Expeditionary Unit/DVIDS,
13; Pfc. Michael Hayes/444th Mobile Public Affairs
Detachment/DVIDS, 14; Mass Communication Specialist
1st Class Cory Asato/US Navy, 17; Sgt. John Crosby/Camp
Atterbury Public Affairs/DVIDS, 18; Lautman/US National
Archives, 20; Shutterstock Images, 21 (top); F Csaba/
Shutterstock Images, 21 (bottom)

ISBN Information
9781503816688 (Reinforced Library Binding)
9781503881365 (Portable Document Format)
9781503882676 (Online Multi-user eBook)
9781503883987 (Electronic Publication)

LCCN 2022951208

Printed in the United States of America

ABOUT THE AUTHOR
Cynthia Kennedy Henzel
has a BS in social studies
education and an MS in
geography. She has worked
as a teacher-educator in
many countries. Currently, she
writes fiction and nonfiction
books and develops education
materials for social studies,
history, science, and ELL
students. She has written
more than 90 books and 150
stories for young people.

CONTENTS

CHAPTER ONE

READY, SET, FIRE!

The soldier stands behind the **mounted** machine gun. The gun is on top of a massive tank. He tries to relax. He is using a **simulator**. The training gun works like a real machine gun. But it does not fire real bullets.

"Gun number one, fire mission," announces the crew leader. This is the soldier's order to prepare to fire.

The soldier moves his hand to the gun's trigger. "Gunner ready," he says.

Through the **sight**, the gunner stares ahead. It feels like his vehicle is bumping down a dusty road.

"Blue truck, left front, 500 meters," the leader says. He is calling out the target, its position, and its approximate distance.

The gunner swings the gun left. "Target identified, 500 meters," he says.

"Fire!"

"On the way," the gunner says. He pulls the trigger. Rattling machine-gun fire fills the air.

There are many kinds of simulators for military training.
Some training centers use headsets to simulate battle.
Others use realistic equipment and large screens.

The soldier steps away from the machine gun simulator, removes the **virtual reality** (VR) headset, and waits for his score.

New VR technology allows machine gun teams to practice without using real ammunition. Using VR, the teams learn to work together. Communication is necessary for a machine-gun crew. Soldiers use standard words to make sure everyone on the team knows what is happening. A mistake could cause confusion about the target. Misunderstanding a command might give an enemy a chance to attack.

A machine gun is an automatic weapon. It fires **cartridges** continually until the gunner releases the trigger or the ammunition runs out. The gun automatically ejects each used cartridge and loads the next one. Other types of guns fire just once each time the gunner pulls the trigger.

PARTS OF A MACHINE GUN

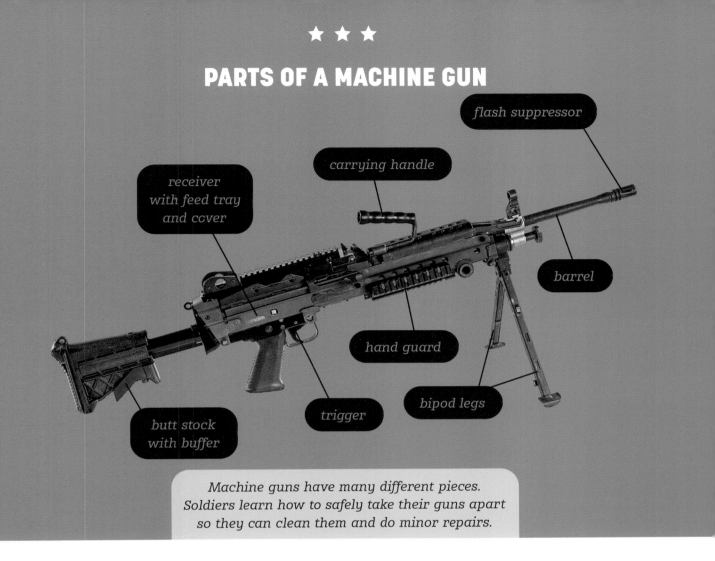

flash suppressor

carrying handle

receiver with feed tray and cover

barrel

hand guard

bipod legs

trigger

butt stock with buffer

Machine guns have many different pieces. Soldiers learn how to safely take their guns apart so they can clean them and do minor repairs.

Hiram Maxim built the first working machine gun in 1884. The US military has used machine guns for more than 100 years. Today, machine guns are divided into light, medium, and heavy guns. Each type of machine gun has its own purpose.

CHAPTER TWO

LIGHT MACHINE GUNS

One common type of light machine gun is the M249. It weighs 18 pounds (8.2 kg). The M249 has **accuracy** similar to a rifle but with the firepower of a machine gun. Having more firepower means machine guns can destroy more enemy targets. While standing, a soldier can fire the weapon held at the shoulder or waist. It has a **bipod** that folds down near the front of the gun to brace the gun on a wall or the ground if needed.

The M249 uses 5.56 mm **rounds**. These are the same size used in the M16—the rifle many soldiers carry. This means the M249 and the M16 can share ammunition. The M249 is fed by a box magazine or a belt. The magazine is a container attached to the gun that holds 30 cartridges stacked side by side. A spring pushes them into the gun. Belts are cartridges that are linked together to form a chain. Belts come in 100- and 200-round pouches. The M249 can shoot up to 850 rounds per minute (rpm).

The M249 has an effective range of about .5 miles (.8 km). That means a soldier can hit a target from about .5 miles away.

Machine guns fire so quickly that the **barrel** overheats. Then the gun jams. Soldiers used water to cool the barrels of early machine guns. The M249 is air-cooled and has a barrel that is easily changed when it gets too hot. A handle on the top of the gun is used to carry the gun or to hold it when changing a hot barrel. A soldier can change the barrel in about seven seconds.

In combat, the M249 uses two different kinds of bullets. Ball rounds are standard and have a green tip. Tracer rounds flash brightly when fired and have an orange tip. They are useful at night to show where a bullet hits.

Light machine guns provide extra firepower to rifle squads. When defending a position, they add the firepower of 10 to 20 rifles without adding extra soldiers. One of the main uses for machine guns is cover fire. Enemies duck or hide when machine guns are firing to avoid getting hit. This lets the US troops move forward into new positions.

The US military began using the M249 in 1984. In the 2020s, it studied possible replacements. The military chose the XM250. The XM250 uses 6.8 mm cartridges, so it works with guns used by the US military and other militaries that are on the same side as the United States. The new gun weighs only 13 pounds (5.9 kg). It has a system that controls when the gun can fire. This system provides more accuracy. A small computer provides the gunner with information on wind and distance to the target.

CHAPTER THREE

MEDIUM MACHINE GUNS

Medium machine guns are often used for cover fire. They use larger cartridges and have a greater range than light machine guns. The M240B is a medium machine gun long used by the US Army, Air Force, Navy, and Coast Guard. It weighs 27.1 pounds (12.3 kg) and fires a 7.62 mm cartridge at up to 950 rpm. The newer M240L is a lightweight version of the M240B. It is made using titanium, which is lighter than other metals. Using titanium saves 5.5 pounds (2.5 kg). This means soldiers have less weight to carry and the gun is easier to handle.

The M240 is usually mounted on a tripod to keep it stable. It can also be mounted on tanks, helicopters, and boats. The M240G is the Marine version of the M240B. The M240G allows the Marines to use one machine gun with different attachments for ground fighting or mounting on vehicles or aircraft. The M240G also has three settings that allow it to fire at different rates.

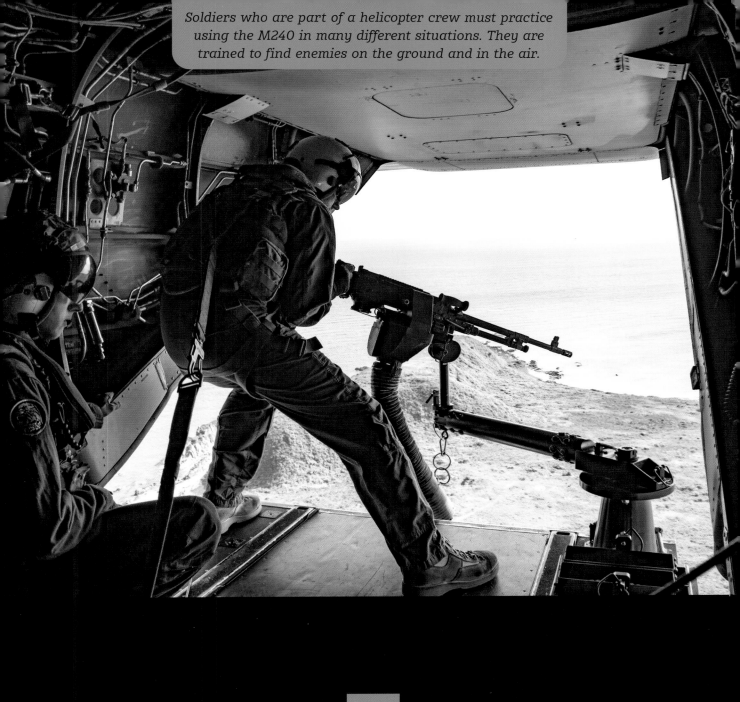

Soldiers who are part of a helicopter crew must practice using the M240 in many different situations. They are trained to find enemies on the ground and in the air.

Machine gun teams train together. Crew members must communicate with one another and understand their jobs to work well together.

More than one person is needed to carry and operate a medium machine gun. For example, a machine gun crew for an M240G has a gunner and an assistant gunner.

The assistant gunner carries extra barrels, helps set up the gun, and changes the barrel. Soldiers can fire 800 rounds in bursts before they should replace the barrel of the gun. But under heavy use, the barrel needs changing every two minutes.

The M240D is often used on aircraft. It has a spade grip. This is a D-shaped handle held by two hands that makes the gun easier to grip. It uses a type of mount that allows the gun to swivel in all directions. When used on a helicopter, it can swivel down to fire at targets on the ground.

TANK GUN

The M240C is used on tanks as a coaxial gun. This type of gun points exactly where the tank's cannon points. The machine gun moves as the cannon moves. The gunner can look through one sight and fire either the machine gun or the cannon, depending on the target. The coaxial gun is used to identify targets before the main cannon fires. This saves the ammunition of the cannon on the tank.

CHAPTER FOUR

HEAVY MACHINE GUNS

One common heavy machine gun in the US military is the M2. It was designed at the end of World War I (1914–1918). This makes it one of the military's oldest weapons still in use. The M2 weighs 84 pounds (38 kg) and is 65 inches (165 cm) long. It fires .50 **caliber** (12.7 mm) rounds at 850 rpm.

The M2 has a spade grip and is normally mounted on the ground or on a vehicle. These huge guns require a crew to operate. Crew members must wheel or carry the gun into position and set it up. They also carry extra barrels and ammunition.

The M2 machine gun is sometimes called the "mother of all machine guns" because it is so powerful.

The MK19 was first used by the US Navy. It is now in use by the US Air Force, Marine Corps, and Army, too.

The M2 provides heavy covering fire so troops can move in or defend against aircraft. The Navy, Army, Air Force, and Marine Corps all use this gun. The newer M2A1 has a flash hider. This makes it harder for the enemy to detect the location of the gun when it is firing, especially at night.

MK19 GRENADE MACHINE GUN

The MK19 Grenade Machine Gun fires 40 mm grenades. The grenades will pierce armor up to 2 inches (5.1 cm) thick. They can destroy helicopters or lightly armored vehicles. The gun can fire up to 60 rpm. The MK19 is not safe to fire at targets closer than 246 feet (75 m) because pieces of the exploding grenades fly in all directions.

The US military used the M2 in World War II (1939–1945).

MACHINE GUN RANGES

GUN	IMAGE	RANGE
M249		.5 miles (.8 km)
M240 with tripod		1.1 miles (1.8 km)
M2		4.2 miles (6.8 km)

Each type of machine gun has a different range. The range tells soldiers how close to a target they need to be when they fire their gun. Bigger guns can hit targets that are farther away.

The US military has used machine guns for decades, but it is always looking for ways to improve them. The process to upgrade machine guns takes years. New weapons are developed by private manufacturers and then tested. Commanders decide how they can use the new guns in the field. New weapons are then manufactured. Troops are trained on the new systems. This process takes time, but it makes certain that the US military continues to have the powerful weapons it needs.

GLOSSARY

accuracy (AK-yur-uh-see) A gun's accuracy measures its ability to hit a target. The machine gun's accuracy was helpful for the soldier.

barrel (BAYR-uhl) The barrel is the tube on the gun through which the bullets travel. Firing a machine gun heats the barrel.

bipod (BY-pod) The two legs that fold out on a machine gun to keep it steady is called the bipod. He set up his machine gun's bipod.

caliber (KAL-uh-bur) The caliber is the size of the ammunition used by a gun. Heavy machine guns use .50 caliber ammunition.

cartridges (KAR-trih-juz) Cartridges are ammunition that contain bullets, gunpowder, and ignition devices. Some machine guns use 5.56 mm cartridges.

mounted (MOWN-tud) Mounted means to be attached to a stand or platform. A lot of machine guns are mounted on top of tanks.

rounds (ROWNDZ) Rounds are ammunition for gunshots. The gun contained five rounds.

sight (SYT) A sight is a device used to help the eye when aiming a gun. She used the sight to make sure her aim was accurate.

simulator (SIM-yuh-lay-tur) A simulator is a machine used for training, with controls that mimic a real vehicle or system. The machine gun simulator was safer than using a real machine gun.

virtual reality (VUR-choo-ul ree-AL-uh-tee) Virtual reality is technology that makes users feel as if they are in a 3D space, which was created on a computer. The soldier used a virtual reality headset to train for combat.

FAST FACTS

★ Machine guns are automatic and continue to fire as long as the trigger is held down.

★ The US Army, Navy, Air Force, Marine Corps, and Coast Guard use machine guns.

★ Machine guns are often fed cartridges with belts.

★ Light machine guns are used by a single person.

★ Medium machine guns such as the M240 are often used to provide covering fire.

★ Medium and heavy machine guns require more than one person to operate.

★ The US military upgrades its machine guns to use the latest technology.

ONE STRIDE FURTHER

★ Machine guns make a big difference in how people fight wars. How do you think machine guns affect the number of troops on the ground? How do they affect the ways soldiers create defenses?

★ The M2 has been used by the US Army since World War I. Why do you think this heavy machine gun has lasted so long as an important weapon?

★ What other weapons changed warfare in the 1900s or 2000s? Choose one weapon and explain the changes it made.

FIND OUT MORE

IN THE LIBRARY

Halls, Kelly Milner. *World War II History for Kids: 500 Facts*. Oakland, CA: Rockridge Press, 2021.

Kenney, Karen L. *Everything World War I*. Washington, DC: National Geographic Kids, 2014.

Lusted, Marcia Amidon. *Missions of the US Army Rangers*. Parker, CO: The Child's World, 2016.

ON THE WEB

Visit our website for links about machine guns:
childsworld.com/links

Note to Parents, Caregivers, Teachers, and Librarians: We routinely verify our Web links to make sure they are safe and active sites. So encourage your readers to check them out!

INDEX